W9-CAO-876

FIESTA!

HUNGARY

An Imprint of Scholastic Library Publishing
Danbury, Connecticut

Published for Grolier
an imprint of Scholastic Library Publishing
Old Sherman Turnpike, Danbury, Connecticut 06816
by Marshall Cavendish Editions
an imprint of Marshall Cavendish International
1 New Industrial Road, Singapore 536196

Copyright © 2004 Times Media Pte Ltd, Singapore
Second Grolier Printing 2006

All rights in this book are reserved. No part of this book may be used or reproduced in any manner
whatsoever or transmitted in any form or by any means, electronic or mechanical, including photocopying,
recording, or any information storage and retrieval system, without written permission from the copyright owner
except in the case of brief quotations embodied in critical articles and reviews. For information, address
the publisher: Scholastic Library Publishing, Old Sherman Turnpike, Danbury, Connecticut 06816.

Set ISBN: 0-7172-5788-6
Volume ISBN: 0-7172-5793-2

Library of Congress Cataloging-in-Publication Data
Hungary.
p. cm.—(Fiesta!)
Summary: Discusses the festivals and holidays of Hungary and how the songs, food,
and traditions associated with these celebrations reflect the culture of the people.
1. Festivals—Hungary—Juvenile literature. 2. Hungary—Social life and customs—Juvenile literature.
[1. Festivals—Hungary. 2. Holidays—Hungary. 3. Hungary—Social life and customs.]
I. Grolier (Firm). II. Fiesta! (Danbury, Conn.)
GT4848.5.A2H85 2004
394.26439—dc21   2003044841

For this volume
Author: Felix Cheong
Editor: Balvinder Sandhu
Designer: Benson Tan
Production: Nor Shidah Haron
Crafts and Recipes produced by Stephen Russell

Printed by Everbest Printing Co. Ltd

Adult supervision advised for all crafts and recipes,
particularly those involving sharp instruments and heat.

CONTENTS

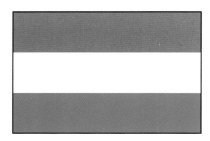

HUNGARY

Hungary is one of the smallest countries in Central Europe. It is even smaller than the state of Indiana. In fact, you can drive from one end of the country to the other in about five hours.

▼ Many Hungarian towns still retain their historic, medieval character. Their buildings date back many centuries. Among these old buildings are **castles,** some already in ruins, that once resisted invading armies. These fortresses can be found at Siklós, Hollókö, and Boldogköváralja.

SLOVAKIA

AUSTRIA

BUDAPEST

Danube

SLOVENIA

Baja

Mohacs

CROATIA

SERBIA

◀ The capital of the Hungarian Republic is **Budapest.** It was formed in 1873 by uniting the towns of Buda and Óbuda on the right bank of the Danube River with Pest on the left bank.

UKRAINE

Debrecen

ROMANIA

▲ The **Danube River** has played an important part in the life of Hungarians for many centuries. It provides freshwater fish and water for irrigation. It is also an important route for transporting heavy goods like oil and timber.

◀ Hungary is famous for its many hot springs on which **thermal baths** have been built. The temperature in the hot springs ranges from 95°F to 195°F. Soaking in the hot springs is said to be good for people suffering from pains like arthritis.

RELIGIONS

The Roman Catholic Church has been a powerful presence in Hungary for many centuries. Many Hungarian customs and folk traditions are linked to various Christian practices.

A figurine of the Virgin Mary and Baby Jesus is a popular fixture in Roman Catholic churches and homes.

The Communist government wanted to promote atheism, which is a belief that there is no God. It banned all religions, took control of church property, and forced church leaders to resign. These restrictions were slowly lifted in the 1980s. When Hungary held its first free elections in forty years in 1990, all controls on religion were finally lifted.

Two-thirds of the Hungarian people belong to the Roman Catholic faith. Nearly a quarter are Protestants, with the Reformed (Calvinist) Church and the Lutheran Church forming the largest Protestant groups. There are also small Greek Catholic and Orthodox congregations.

HUNGARY has been a Christian nation since the tenth century, when King Stephen I converted his people to Roman Catholicism. Christianity is so much a part of the Hungarian way of life that many folk traditions have their origin in religious practices. In fact, until 1948, when the Communists took over the country, the Roman Catholic Church was in charge of running most schools.

Hungarian children sometimes wear a pendant of Catholic design such as this.

GREETINGS FROM **HUNGARY!**

People from Hungary call themselves Magyars. They are descendants of warrior horsemen who migrated from Central Asia more than one thousand years ago. Their language has developed over the years into the tongue now known as Hungarian. But for centuries after the reign of King Stephen I Latin, as the official language of the Catholic Church, was also the official Hungarian language. It was only in the last five hundred years that Hungarian became widely accepted as the official language. There are forty-four characters in the Hungarian alphabet, compared with twenty-six in the English one. The Hungarian language borrows many words from German, Latin, Turkish, and the Slavic languages. Today many Hungarians speak a second language, such as German or English.

How do you say...

Hello
Szervusz

Good Morning
Jó reggelt

How are you?
Hogy van?

Goodbye
Viszontlátásra

Thank you
Köszönöm

BUSÓJÁRÁS

A week before the season of Lent people in the town of Mohács take part in an unusual festival during which celebrations include folk dancing, musical performances, and the procession of the busós.

One of the most spectacular folk festivals in the country is the Busójárás, or the walk of the legendary busó monsters. Held in the Mohács district, the festival takes place the week before Ash Wednesday. It has no links to Christian practices. Instead, it originated from ancient celebrations of the arrival of spring.

On the Friday before Ash Wednesday children gather and wander the streets wearing old clothes and stocking masks over their faces.

They carry bags of flour or stockings filled with sawdust, and they playfully hit any woman or girl who cannot outrun them. No harm is intended, and no one is hurt.

To keep the festivities lively, the city of Mohács also hosts folk dancing and music during the weekend. There are also food and arts and crafts stalls lined along the streets.

During the procession on Busójárás men wear jackets or vests made of sheepskin.

Busójárás celebrations ends with a cannon firing rags with oil and gunpowder into the sky.

What everyone must be eagerly waiting for is the procession of the *busós* — the men of Mohács who dress up in sheepskin jackets or vests, black boots, and horned wooden masks. Each hand-painted mask has a scary expression that is believed to drive away evil spirits.

It is also a reminder of the time during the sixteenth and seventeenth century when the *busós* scared away the Turkish soldiers threatening to invade their homes. Every *busó* carries either a large wooden noisemaker or a cowbell.

At twelve o'clock in the afternoon on Sunday all the *busós* cross the Danube River in their boats and make their way as a magnificent procession to the main square.

Thousands of locals, tourists, and visitors are assembled there to catch the action. The *busós* dance around a huge bonfire, creating a racket with their noisemakers.

The carnival ends with the burning of a straw puppet to symbolize the end of winter. A cannon stuffed with oily rags and gunpowder is then fired into the sky.

The men of Mohács wear black boots during the procession on Busójárás.

MAKE A BUSÓ MASK

YOU WILL NEED
A 16-inch by 24-inch sheet of construction paper
Adhesive tape
PVC glue
Poster paint

1 Make a cylindrical shape with the sheet of construction paper.

2 Put it over your head. Hold it firmly, and ask a friend to mark out the position of your eyes and mouth on the paper. Draw a design on the paper to fit around the position of your eyes and mouth.

3 Open up the mask, and neatly cut out the eye and mouth holes.

4 Roll the mask back into shape, and use strong adhesive tape or PVC glue to hold it together.

5 Paint your mask in the *busó* colors.

9

BUDAPEST SPRING FESTIVAL

The Budapest Spring Festival is one of the newest festivals in Hungary. It takes place in the last two weeks of March and has become "the festival of festivals," the cultural highlight in the Hungarian calendar.

In 1981 the Budapest Spring Festival was introduced for two reasons. They were to promote Budapest as a modern cultural city and to attract more visitors to the city.

The first festival staged eighty events over a period of ten days at such grand places as the Academy of Music and the breathaking Castle District.

The Spring Festival is generally a platform to showcase the city's cultural diversity through music and display the melting pot of different cultural styles that make up the city of Budapest.

The festival has been growing in size over the years. It now invites famous musicians from around the world to perform and also draws numerous tourists from all over Europe, who visit the city just to take in this totally unique experience.

The program offers a

wide selection of performances catering to different tastes. They range from classical music, ballet and opera, to pop music and jazz, to folk music programs, and exhibitions.

Recently the festival has featured performances by some famous classical musicians, such as the talented Russian pianist Lazar Berman and the Hungarian violinist Andras Keller.

During the festival there are several concerts for which you need to dress up appropriately, but there are also outdoor events at which you can have a picnic with your family and enjoy the cool spring air.

During the Budapest Spring Festival musicians showcase their talents using a variety of instruments, including the drums, trumpet, French horn, and violin.

SÁNDOR PETŐFI

Sándor Petőfi was a popular poet and one of the leaders of the famous 1848 revolution. Although he died in 1849, he remains a national hero and martyr, and his poetry is still taught in schools throughout Hungary today.

Sándor Petőfi was born in 1823 in Kiskôrös, a town south of Budapest. Although he did not do very well in school, he developed a strong interest in drama and literature. He started writing poetry and had his first poem published when he was just nineteen.

As a young man, Petőfi did a lot of traveling, mostly on foot, throughout the countryside. Here he saw for himself how poor and ill-treated his fellow Hungarians were. And so he began writing many poems with the themes of love and liberty.

During the old days a quill (above) was used as a pen, after being dipped into an inkpot (right).

In his poems he described the joys and sorrows of the common people, using everyday language so that everyone was able to understand his message. He also talked about married love and family life. Most of all, he talked about freeing his beloved Hungary from Austrian rule.

In 1846 Petőfi put his words into action. He formed the urban-based Society of 10, a group of young Hungarians who, like him, were eager for change in their country.

Later on, he stood on the steps of the National Museum in Pest and recited his poem "National Song," urging Hungarians to rise up against Austrian rule. Gradually this led to the outbreak of the revolution in 1848.

Petőfi became assistant to the general leading the revolt. A year later, when the revolution ended, Petőfi was one of many Hungarians who was killed in battle against the invading Russian army, which was called in to help by the Austrians. However, no one witnessed Petőfi's death, and his body was never found.

It seems that Petőfi had a premonition of how his death would occur. One of his poems, "One Thought Torments Me," contains these lines:

Today Petőfi's poetry is taught in schools all over Hungary. One of his most famous poems is "Freedom, Love," which most people in Hungary know by heart.

Today his memory is preserved in hundreds of street names, statues, and plaques all over Hungary. In fact, there is even a radio station named for him in Budapest.

The famous Petőfi statue in Budapest shows the poet with his right arm raised, which makes it seem as if he is calling for his countrymen to rise up in action. In his left hand he holds a scroll,

for the pride of an independent Hungary. As he wrote in his famous poem "National Song":

On your feet, Magyar, the homeland calls
Now is the time, it's now or never
Shall we be slaves or free men?
That's the question, answer now!
God of the Hungarians
We swear
We swear that slaves
We shall be no more.

When Sándor Petőfi and his army of men fought in the Hungarian revolution, they were armed with weapons such as this.

Let me die on that battlefield.
Let my young blood flow there from my heart...
And above my corpse wheezing horses will trot off
To the well-deserved victory, leaving me trampled to death.

which probably contains the words to one of his many famous poems.

Many Hungarians are able to identify with Petőfi because his poetry speaks

13

EASTER

Easter is a time for Christians to remember that Jesus Christ died on the cross for their sins and that he rose from the dead three days later. It is celebrated slightly differently in Hungary than in other Christian countries.

Easter is a two-day holiday in Hungary. Its observance is unusual among European countries because its practice is part Christian and part folk tradition.

What is different is the ritual of sprinkling, practiced by many people across the whole country. Sprinkling probably arose from a belief in the cleansing, healing, and fertility effects of water.

Palm leaves are used to represent Palm Sunday, the start of Holy Week for Christians, which ends with Easter.

On Easter Monday boys and young men wake up early to visit their female relatives, neighbors, and friends. They leave the house in the morning, and these visits usually last the whole day.

In the past the boys would playfully drag the girls to the well and, using pails, pour water on them. Or they would take the girls to the river and drench them. This meant that the girls had to change their clothes

CREATE A HUNGARIAN EASTER EGG

YOU WILL NEED
1 egg
Poster paint
Paintbrush
Needle

3 With a needle gently scratch the design you want on the egg surface.

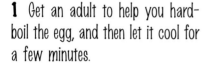

1 Get an adult to help you hard-boil the egg, and then let it cool for a few minutes.

2 Paint the whole egg, preferably using only one color, such as red.

4 You can either follow traditional Hungarian folk-art patterns such as flowers or horseshoes, which are more fashionable these days.

after each sprinkling.

These days the boys tend to sprinkle cologne rather than water on the girls. And instead of folk costumes, the girls put on casual clothes, and they treat the boys who sprinkle them to desserts, drinks, as well as personally hand-painted and decorated eggs.

There is also usually competition among the girls as to who gets the most sprinkles. By the time the celebrations come to an end in the evening, with the traditional Easter feast of baked ham and boiled eggs, you can probably smell more than a dozen different types of cologne on the girls!

LUCA DAY

December 13 is the name day of Saint Luca (or Lucia in Italian), a saint's day especially for women and girls. Because her name is associated with light Saint Luca is the patron saint of the blind. She is also one of the patron saints of virgins.

BORN IN THE year 304 in a small town in Sicily, Italy, Luca came from a wealthy family. She lived during a period when the early Christians suffered hardship and persecution by the Romans for their beliefs.

But Luca was courageous and was not afraid of the Romans. She helped her fellow Christians by bringing food to those hiding in dark underground tunnels. She was eventually found out and sentenced to death.

Even though Saint Luca was Italian, many Christian countries celebrate her feast day, including Sweden, Norway, and Hungary. And each country has its own way of remembering Saint Luca.

In Hungary there are several folk traditions linked with the name day of Saint Luca. One of them is the making of the Luca chair. It looks like a step stool rather than a chair, with no arms or backrest. It is made by hand from seven different kinds of wood.

The chair has to be completed in time for Christmas Eve so that you can take it with you to church on that day. It is said that if you stand on this chair during midnight mass, you can see the witches in the crowd!

However, immediately afterward you must run home and throw the chair into the fire, for it is believed that the witches will come after any owner of a Luca chair.

On this day females are not allowed to work. And girls are fond of making Luca slips, which are little pieces of paper

with a boy's name written on each one of them. These slips are then rolled into dumpling dough.

During the cooking process the first dumpling to rise to the surface of the soup contains the slip of paper with the name of the girl's future husband.

Another tradition is the sowing of Luca wheat. Farmers plant exactly one hundred grains of wheat in a container. How they sprout by Christmas indicates how the following year's crop will do.

JOHNNY FLOATING

The ceremony of Johnny Floating is a European festival celebrated every year in the Hungarian town of Baja on May 15, the eve of Saint John's name day.

John Wolflin was born in 1345 in Bohemia. Legend has it that he was sentenced to death by the king because he refused to reveal what the queen said during confession.

As a priest, John had taken a vow to keep all confessions a secret.

On the night of his death the people of Prague were said to witness seven stars floating on the Moldau River at the spot where he drowned.

Since then those who live by the river, including the Hungarian town Baja, have adopted Saint John as their patron saint.

Celebrations in Baja begin with Mass at Saint John Chapel. After Mass the statue of Saint John, decorated with flowers, is carried in a procession to

During the procession that takes place on Johnny Floating, lighted torches are carried on Sugovica Bridge.

the Sugovica River.

It is placed on a boat that slowly makes its way to Sugovica Bridge, flanked by barges, canoes, and kayaks, each carrying lighted torches. Burning pitch wreaths can also be found floating on the river, a reminder of the miracle of floating stars.

The festivities then continue in the town center, where people dance happily to folk music and feast on traditional dishes such as fish soup.

Hungarians commemorate Johnny Floating even though Saint John was not Hungarian.

HALÁSZLÉ (FISH SOUP)

Hungarians enjoy soup with their meals. One traditional soup that is popular with many is fish soup. You may need an adult's help in preparing this dish.

SERVES 6 to 8

12 cups fish stock
1 tbsp paprika
3 pounds freshwater fish fillets, cut into
bite-sized chunks and seasoned with salt
3 peppers, chopped (green and yellow)
1 tomato, skinned and chopped
Salt and pepper
$1/4$ sliced green bell pepper

1 Bring the stock to a boil, and stir in the paprika. Let it simmer for a minute.

2 Add pieces of fish and their roe (if available), the chopped tomato and peppers, and cook over high heat for 20 minutes.

3 Don't stir the soup, or you will break the fish. Just tilt the pan from side to side to keep the pieces of fish from sticking.

4 When it is ready to serve, season to taste, and garnish with sliced green peppers.

19

KING STEPHEN I

King Stephen I is regarded as Hungary's greatest king.
For converting his people to the Roman Catholic faith,
he was canonized Saint Stephen after his death.

KNOWN AS the Apostle of Hungary, King Stephen I came to the throne on Christmas Day in the year 1000, when he was twenty-three years old. Up to that point in their history the Magyar people had often lived under foreign occupation, experiencing much hardship and many terrible wars.

Married to a German princess, King Stephen I modeled his kingdom on that of the German monarchy. First, to unite all the tribes of his country into one nation, he seized lands owned by clan chiefs. He divided it into counties, each protected by fortified castles, and appointed royal officials to rule over them.

King Stephen I then set about converting his people to the Roman Catholic faith, ordering one in every ten villages to build a church. He laid down Hungary's first written laws and persuaded the Magyars to adopt European customs.

He also invited scholars, artists, and craftsmen to settle in Hungary so that they could pass on their skills to the people of his country.

King Stephen I was a very kind ruler. He always listened to his people, and he was always willing to help the poor.

Legend has it that one day while he was in disguise distributing alms to the poor, a group of beggars crowded around him. They knocked him down, pulled at his beard and hair, and stole his money. He did not get angry at all but instead renewed his vow never to refuse alms to any poor person who asked him.

King Stephen I died at the age of sixty-three in the year 1038. The Roman Catholic Church later canonized him. His crown, which was presented to him by Pope Sylvester II, has remained throughout the centuries as the sacred symbol of Hungarian national existence.

SAINT STEPHEN'S DAY

August 20 is the most important public holiday on the Hungarian calendar. It commemorates Saint Stephen, the founder of the Hungarian nation. Celebrations include parades, folk dancing, and a fireworks display.

Folk dancing takes place on Saint Stephen's Day, and women dress in the appropriate oufits for it.

August 20 celebrates the Feast of Saint Stephen, patron saint and founder of the Hungarian nation. In the Communist era between 1948 and 1989 the leaders wanted people to forget the importance of Saint Stephen's Day. So they re-named it Constitution Day, since August 20 was the date the Communists came into power.

The Communists also planned for it to be a day to celebrate the summer harvest, which was called "the day of the bread." In the past a village priest would bless a freshly baked

During Communist rule a loaf of bread with a ribbon in national colors around it was cut on Saint Stephen's Day.

loaf of bread as an offering to God.

The Communists had one of their leaders do a similar rite, which involved cutting a loaf with a ribbon in national colors tied around it.

But this renaming did not work. The Hungarian peope still prefered the day to be a remembrance of Saint Stephen as the father of their nation.

When the Communists' reign finally ended in 1989, Saint Stephen's Day was restored and recognized once again for its national and religious importance.

The day's highlight is the solemn procession in which the mummified hand of Saint Stephen is carried from the Basilica of Esztergom through the streets of Budapest.

On the same day the colorful Flower Festival entertains crowds in the city of Debrecen. Across the country the day is marked by folk dancing, sporting events, and various parades.

What must not be missed is a spectacular display of fireworks that completes this special day's celebrations.

Hungarians are proud of Saint Stephen and wear their national costume on August 20.

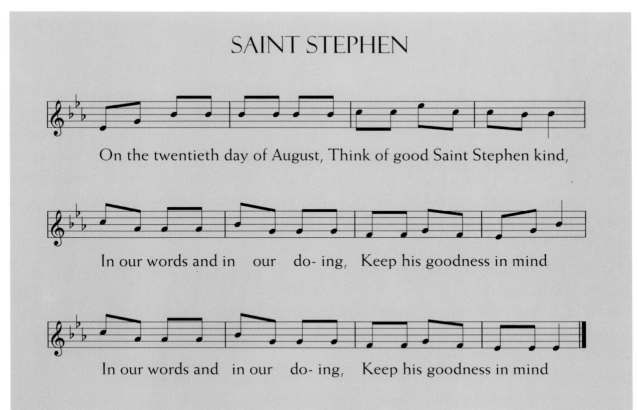

SAINT STEPHEN

On the twentieth day of August, Think of good Saint Stephen kind,

In our words and in our do- ing, Keep his goodness in mind

In our words and in our do- ing, Keep his goodness in mind

23

CHRISTMAS

In Hungary Christmas is a two-day holiday. For many children the festive mood begins with Advent, when they get an Advent calendar to help them count down excitedly to Christmas Day.

In preparation for the festive season households hang Christmas wreaths on their front doors.

When shops, schools and offices, and almost all homes across the country start putting up Christmas wreaths on their front doors, you know that Advent is here.

To get themselves excited about the festive season, Hungarian children get little Advent calendars to help them count down to December 25. They also receive gifts or sweets for each day leading to Christmas Day.

Christmas in Hungary is celebrated differently than in other countries. For instance, children hang boots in the windows, just as stockings are hung by the fireplace elsewhere in the world. And this is done on December 6, not on Christmas Eve.

That is because the Hungarian Santa, Mikulas, visits children on that day, the name day of Saint Nicholas. If children have behaved themselves the past year, their boot is filled with goodies such as candy and chocolate Mikulas

Advent candles are a popular way for Hungarians to count down to Christmas.

figurines. If they have been naughty, their boot will have a switch, usually with a devil figure attached to it.

Another folk tradition is the Bethlehem play. A few days before Christmas groups of boys go from house to house around the city, carrying a model of the nativity. Dressed in costumes, they put on a musical play about the birth of Jesus Christ. This

unique tradition dates back four hundred years.

Christmas trees are never decorated before the Holy Night in Hungary. Instead, most families decorate them together on Christmas Eve.

The menu for this night features fried fish, fish soup, roast goose with red cabbage, and tortes. For dessert there is an assortment of cookies and *beigli*, the traditional poppy-seed and nut rolls.

After the feast family members gather around the Christmas tree to sing carols and unwrap their presents.

On Boxing Day Hungarians visit family and friends, sometimes traveling to another town. The menu usually consists of stuffed cabbage, a dish specially prepared the week before.

Popping Christmas crackers is one of the ways Christmas is celebrated in Hungary.

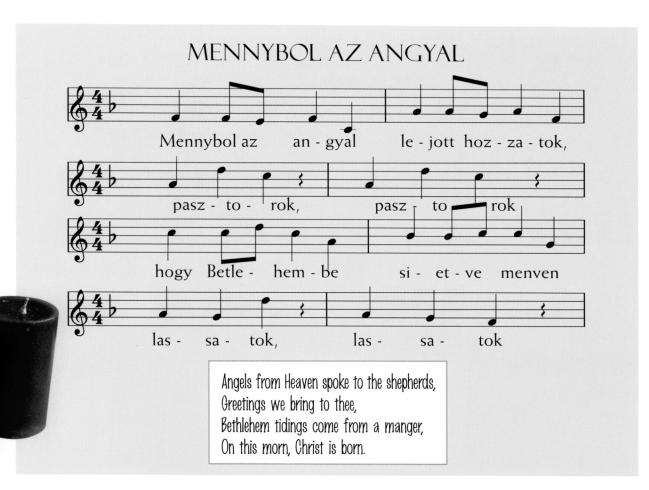

MENNYBOL AZ ANGYAL

Mennybol az an - gyal le - jott hoz - za - tok,

pasz - to - rok, pasz - to - rok

hogy Betle - hem - be si - et - ve menven

las - sa - tok, las - sa - tok

Angels from Heaven spoke to the shepherds,
Greetings we bring to thee,
Bethlehem tidings come from a manger,
On this morn, Christ is born.

New Year's Eve

In Hungary December 31 is also a time to remember God's blessings. Traditional dishes such as cold pork and poppy-seed and nut rolls are served on this day.

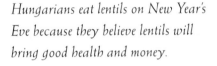

The Hungarian name for New Year's Eve is Szilveszter, or Sylvester, for a saint's name day. Although it is a working day, the holiday mood still lingers from Christmas.

Immediately after work people join their families and friends in feasting and merrymaking. As the New Year approaches, you can hear lively music from bustling street parades, live concerts, and parties.

The traditional dishes prepared are cold pork in aspic, sausages with horseradish and mustard, and poppy-seed and nut rolls. After midnight roast pork is also served.

But before diving into the meal, Hungarians put a stalk of green wheat (which is sown before Christmas), a prayer book,

Hungarians eat lentils on New Year's Eve because they believe lentils will bring good health and money.

and a purse full of money on the dining table. These items are an offering of thanks to God that will also bring about his blessings for the New Year.

When midnight finally arrives, many Hungarians

Colorful streamers are used to create a party atmosphere on New Year's Eve.

celebrate by opening champagne bottles, singing the country's national anthem, and greeting each other with *"buek,"* which means "Happy New Year."

Like most festivals in Hungary, there are several folk beliefs linked to Szilveszter. For instance, the way you spend the last day of the year is how you will spend the coming year. So you should not feel sad or lonely or fall ill. But you should eat something sweet for the first bite of the year. And the first kiss you get is important too, for that is the person you will love the next year.

A stalk of green wheat is one of the items that Hungarians offer as a thanks to God.

Other beliefs relate to the right kind of food to be eaten. For example, you should not eat fish, since the fish might swim away with your luck.

Similarly, you should not eat chicken, for it might bury your luck. If you want to be rich and healthy, you should eat a dish of lentils and pork.

NAME DAYS

It is a Hungarian custom to celebrate "name days"; they are even more important than birthdays. Each day of the year is given a certain Christian name. Some of these names are based on feast days of saints, while others are taken from ordinary names like László, Zoltán, or Zsuzsanna. Name days are often celebrated with flowers, gifts, and dinners with the family.

Once the clock strikes midnight, the party starts, and party poppers are used to ring in the new year.

27

BEIGLI (POPPY-SEED AND NUT ROLL)

This dish is a traditional favorite among Hungarians on New Year's Eve. Learn how to make this delicious pastry, and include it on the menu for your next New Year's Eve party!

YOU WILL NEED

(For pastry)
10 oz plain flour
7 oz butter
$^3/_4$ oz yeast
2 egg yolks
4 tbsp milk
A pinch of salt

(For filling)
10 oz ground walnuts
5 tbsp milk
9 oz sugar
4 tbsp raisins
3 oz butter

6 Roll out the two loaves of pastry to knife-blade thickness and a rectangular shape. Spread half the filling on each rectangle.

7 Roll up each piece like a swiss roll.

8 Place them on a greased baking sheet, and let them stand for 10 minutes.

1 Crumble flour and butter together in a bowl.

2 Make a well in the center; add in the sugar, salt, and yolks.

3 Dissolve yeast in four tablespoons of warm milk; add to mixture in bowl. Work the dough well until smooth.

4 Shape it into two loaves, and let them rest for 30 minutes. In the meantime, prepare the filling.

5 Heat sugar and milk, add nuts, and stir over low heat for a few minutes. Take it off the heat, beat in the butter and raisins, and let it cool.

9 Brush them with egg white.

10 Bake in hot oven for 30 to 40 minutes.

11 Cool rolls, and serve sliced into $\frac{1}{2}$ inch thickness.

NATIONAL DAY

March 15 is the anniversary of the outbreak of the 1848 revolution and war of independence. This day is an important occasion for Hungarians to express their patriotism and celebrate their country's independence.

The Hungarian coat of arms is a reminder of the country's independence.

Hungary was part of the Habsburg Empire ruled by Austria during the 19th century. The majority of the Magyar people did not own any land and were very poor. Therefore most of them had to work long days on the farms and were frequently mistreated by the rich landowners.

A group of patriotic Hungarians wanted to bring about social changes in their country. Among the list of reforms was education for the poor.

More importantly, they wanted independence from neighboring Austria.

This led to a revolt in 1848 in which many Hungarians were killed. This war of independence lasted a year.

Today Hungarians commemorate the 1848 revolution on March 15 with military parades. Public buildings such as the National Museum in Budapest are decked in the Hungarian national colors of red, white, and green. A rally and a performance also take place here.

People gather for rallies outside the National Museum and at the Petőfi Statue. They take time to remember the heroes who sacrificed their lives in that fateful war.

Hungarians fought for independence and wanted to form their own country because they were forced to work very hard on the farms for very low wages.

WORDS TO KNOW

Advent: The period before Christmas, when Christians prepare to celebrate the birth of Jesus Christ.

Arthritis: A painful stiffness and swelling in and around the joints.

Ash Wednesday: The day that marks the beginning of Lent.

Atheism: The belief that there is no God.

Canonize: The process by which the Roman Catholic Church recognizes the good deeds of a holy person and gives him or her the status of a saint.

Communist: A person who believes in a classless society and that everyone has an equal share in all property and works toward a common good.

Democracy: A system of government in which citizens have a chance to vote once every four to five years for whom they want to run their country.

Lent: A period of repentance in remembrance of the death and resurrection of Jesus Christ. It starts on Ash Wednesday and ends on Easter Sunday.

Mass: The Roman Catholic Church service in which the ritual of Holy Communion takes place.

Miracle: An event or occurrence that cannot be explained by science and is believed by Christians to be the work of God.

Patron saint: A saint who is believed to take care of a particular group of people, often because his or her life was linked with that group.

Protestant: A member of one of the churches that make up the main branches of Christianity.

Rite: A procedure that is part of a religious event.

Roman Catholic: A member of the Roman Catholic Church. The head of the church is the pope.

ACKNOWLEDGMENTS

WITH THANKS TO:
Yumi Ng, Daphne Rodrigues, Alan Tay, and Yeo Puay Khoon for the loan of artifacts used in the production of this book.

PHOTOGRAPHS BY:
International Photobank (cover), Sam Yeo (p. 8 top, p. 12 all, p. 18 top, p. 24 bottom, p. 25, p. 26 all), Yu Hui Ying (all other images).

ILLUSTRATIONS BY:
Jailani Basari (p. 1), Amy Ong (pp. 4-5), Enrico Sallustio (p. 7), Ong Lay Keng (p. 17 and p. 21), Cake (p. 30).

SET CONTENTS